Museworks

Poems of Blood, Love and of Passion

To Paul
Best Wishes!
Alex

Alexander Wallis

Cover & art by Duncan Clarke
Poetry page art by Phil Ives
Fiction page art by Ellrano

BloodRedStar

BloodRedStar Publications

This first edition published in Great Britain in 2022 by BloodRedStar Publications

Enquiries to: thewayknight@outlook.com

ISBN: 9798829842574

INTRODUCTION

A poet wanders through the ruins of experience and hopes to glean wisdom from the mouths of statues found there. Catching an insight, the poet scribbles it down and offers it to the world with tentative flourish.

I offer here the findings of my own expeditions into dreams, memory, and imagination. Reflections polished into a museum of thoughts and given a grand opening in book form.

Feel free to climb on the displays and take photos.

Alexander

POETRY

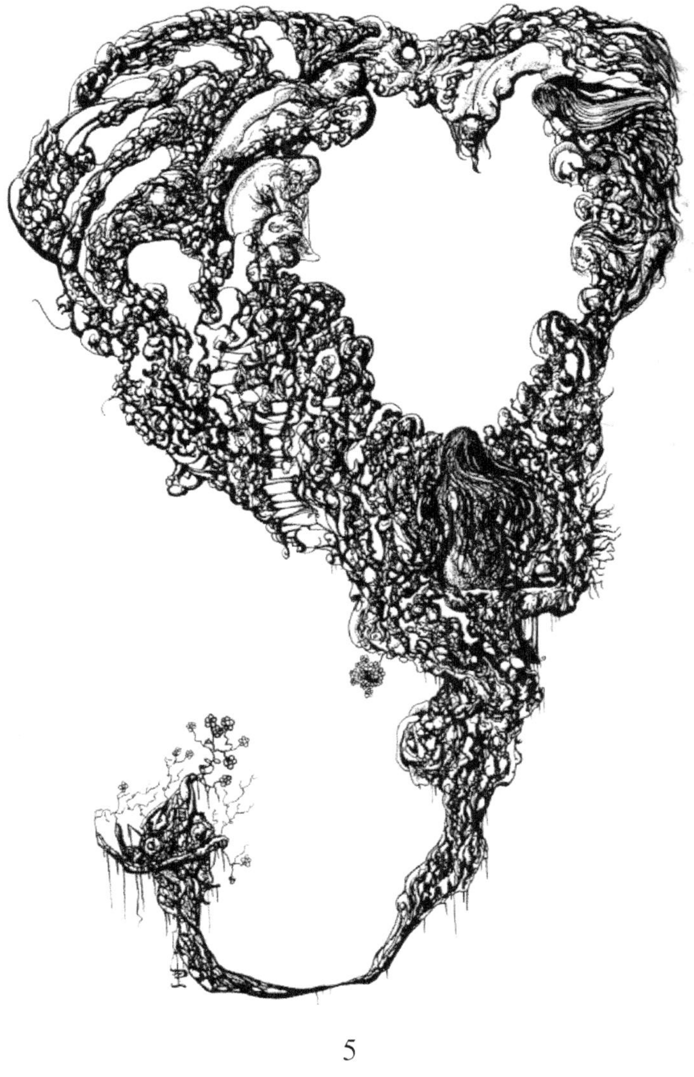

A SURVIVOR

Battlefield drenched in mist
Clefts of mud make cliffs
While warriors on the brink
Of life, croak prayers and sink
Gratefully to death's abyss.

Distance away - a survivor
Sword too heavy to lift
Amid the debris drifts
Shield fragments scattered
Like the scars upon his fists.

Though weather groans and weeps
For the foes dead at his feet,
No emotion makes him shrink
Nor feeling through his visor blinks.

Beyond sturdy armour
What secrets sleep?
A heart forever shielded
Or is nothing left beneath?

SADNESS WARMS THE HEART

Sadness is your friend and lover
Every moment she will smother,
Never let you love another
Sadness warms the heart.

Have no doubt that you will meet her
Hear her make the sad songs sweeter,
Fleeting smiles will not defeat her
Sadness warms the heart.

Her touch will make bad memories linger
Your tears are gems upon her fingers,
She swears that you will never part
Sadness warms the heart.

Sadness will be yours forever
She loves the time you spend together,
You'll never hear her cry or complain
She says kiss me and kiss me again.

PLACEBO PRISONER

When your shoe hits the street
You enter a contract
Written in the concrete.
When you take their routes
You are numbered meat
Self-direction obsolete.

On the web you feel like air
Shopping for something
Some elusive content.
When you're dead
You'll linger there.
Still in algorithm's snare.

None of the maps are true.
Truth is not in a shopping cart
It's here. And inside you
It's a state of heart
Not a change of face.
Will you let it find you?

HOW TO KNOW ME

Give me slow conversation
Considered observations,
Speak as if your every word
Was honed for the occasion.

Surprise me with your questions
Discard all vain pretentions
Let's exchange authentically
Not spit out misconceptions.

Discard trivial recollection
For meaningful connection,
We'll see each other truthfully
When deep in real reflection.

Let's combine imaginations
Acknowledge limitations
Friends exploring heart-to-heart
Don't hide their imperfections.

HOLIDAY

Then we were caked in flesh
Stars buried in incarnation
Memories lost but a lingering knowledge
This skin just a vacation

In tears we baptise our human state
In blood hot through the gates
Emotions too fierce to relate
Finite perceptions with which to navigate

Experience pouring
Souls longing
Trauma pollutes us
Relationships dry or dilute us

We touch other stars
Some bloom with recognition
They light us for a time
Casting cherished shadows long behind

Take firm my hands
Hurts are just scabs of our mortal condition
In velocity of light be thrown
'Til we return to our cosmic position

THE DEAD OF NIGHT

In the dark the nymphs are musing,
Prowling, smiling and approving
Of the shadows that are moving
Slowly in the dead of night.

And the creak of wood is thunder,
As she sighs and laughs in wonder
Her expressions are his plunder
Breaths held in the dead of night.

Can you hear her sweetly weeping?
Deepness of her lover speaking
In the morn they refrain speaking
Eyes still in the dead of night.

DEEP DIVE

Leagues below the ocean deep
'Neath catacombs, a Dark God sleeps.
Sunken wrecks lay at his feet
Alien scenes from his mind creep.

His coffin glows peculiar stones
And our weak world is now his home.
Before men crawled, came his descent
And when he stirs, comes our torment.

As he snores, he tastes the frantic
Dumping of huge tons of plastic
Discharge, sewage, oil, pollution
Wrack his dreams of retribution.

His tentacles begin to quiver
Apocalyptic waves of litter
Destroy all life beneath the ocean
One alien eye threatens to open.

So deep the ignorance and malice
A plastic bag finds the Dark God's palace
Where the whales would dive and splash
In a stream of man-made trash.

In his bed we've poured our waste
Too late now, we've sealed our fate
For in the stars, death is foretold
When he awakes and eats our souls.

THE VAMPIRE QUEEN LENORA

From the ancient castle sung
The vampire queen, Lenora.
Her song evoked the tragedies
Of every soul who saw her.

Ravens were her company
And spiders were her spies,
And by her side a blind man stood
Whose blood trailed from his eyes.

'Oh, Lenora. Marry me!'
Her knight, Cervantes, dared.
He had scaled the battlements
Black roses in his hair.

'Be not alone, for I have roamed
The kingdom in thy name.
Of all your knights, I love you best.
Deny me not - for shame.'

Lenora's lips revealed her teeth
Her eyes sad as the grave,
'Cervantes, do you see the man
Upon the palisade?'

Cervantes looked but only saw
A titan hewn from rock
'But that is just a statue
And it has a cherub's cock.'

The queen picked out a single rose
Plucked petals to the bone
'I must possess me such a man
Be he god or hewn from stone.'

'Milady,' her brave champion growled
'No perfect thing can love
It is endearing weakness, which
Stirs feelings from above.'

Lenora kissed her knight, 'My friend,
I do treasure your valour
But I must find the perfect king
Such as stands upon yon tower.'

And so, the knight stood lowly watch
While Lenora's voice took flight
Both with longing in their hearts
In the dark song of the night.

MACHINE

The city outskirts are still flesh
Beyond the wall, few humans left.
Mobile apps keep them asleep
While replicants play kill-and-seek.

Most nights I try to self-repair
Surfing through the old malware.
I watch the people walk about
My dereliction freaks them out.

C.I.N.D.Y. (my operating system)
Insists I should report my position.
I cut her voice with a small incision
Ain't going back to that android prison.

I've been offline before but
They re-acquired and plugged me back in.
Since then, the data-sniffing's thin
I snorted some apps from a broken sim.

Hard to say now, what is real?
Lost some memories in a three-for-one deal
Can someone tell me how I feel?
It should display on my frontal lobe wheel.

Now I live from fix to fix.
Not looking for pity, but d'you have a hit?
Just in a dry patch. Everything's sweet.
Can you spare a little data 'til I'm back on my feet?

SEE HER DANCE

See her dance
With that sheet
Sailing wind
Precious feet

Tiny stones
Stick her toes
Flapping silk
Wind bellows

And her smile
Doesn't care
That her partner
Is the air

For her soul
Is in the moves
The fulsome wind
Shows he approves

And her shriek
Is a laugh
And her smile
Breaks your heart

Is it God
Snatched from a line
Or only she
Who is divine?

GOD'S WORK, LADS

'God's work, lads,'
The sergeant said,
After Parker and Jones
Were shot in the head.

'Fall asleep on your watch
And the angels forsake you.
We've devils to kill
And a fortress to get to!'

'Your rifles are holy,'
The Chaplain agreed.
'The Lord's own spears
Against Napoleon's greed!'

So, we marched until
Our boots ran red
And we ran our drills
So's not to end up dead.

Sunday and the valley bled
Lit by blasts of lightning.
Men felled by sabre and shot
In the vicious fighting.

'Jesus save us!'
The sergeant said
Right before a musket
Blew apart his head.

'Heaven's above!'
The chaplain cried
As he attempted to shovel
His guts back inside.

Angels were there
In the glorious sounds
I heard the crack of their wings
As death dragged me down.

COURT OF DREAMS

When the toys retire today,
All the safe things drip away.
Holding tight to my blue sheets,
I struggle with the urge to sleep.

Eyelids sink and I despair
'Please, no nightmares,' is my prayer.
Shadows bite away the walls
From my room a cavern sprawls.

Here there is no safe relief
Gone are parents, teachers, police.
Adults have abandoned me,
A prisoner in the Court of Dreams.

In a temple, set me free
Things a child should never see
Old things wriggle after me
To feed their violent ceremonies.

Something bad is waiting ahead
Its many names cannot be said
A pyramid its crypt and yet
It has never died - but slept.

I awake with no relief
My lids stuck shut I cannot see.
My sight remains inside the dream
My body cannot move. I scream!

'Dad!' I shout and at the word
The thing inside the crypt has stirred
The prisoned horror now unsealed
My hiding place has been revealed.

My terror is the food it craves
My sticky eyelids form a cage.
If the monster tastes my pain
I'll never see my friends again.

With force, my eyes erupt so wide
Like gasping air. The dream subsides.
And sunlight cures me with its glow
But now the shadows wait and know.

CREATURES

'Her gaze turns men to stone,' they warned
'Like shadows they become.'
And in their faces, I could see
They hoped I'd be the one.

I drank my wine and listened
To the stories each man spun
Fear cut at the air they breathed
Was heard on every tongue.

I drained the cup and felt them eye
My muscles and my scars
To them a hero's legacy
To me - survivor's marks.

A warrior's courage might yet hold,
Where lesser men had failed.
'Slay the creature,' I was told
'Avoid her eyes and tail!'

As sunlight withered, I designed
To pray and gird my loins
I took some bread but left behind
Their offering of coins.

A ravine was the creature's lair
A place of ash, so old.
Trees bent at the sight of me
Stood statues on the road.

A cave offered its greedy mouth
I raised my battered shield
With each step, in night I crept
Sought the truth to be revealed.

In the gloom a creature hissed
A trembling feral youth
Crouching to defend herself
She threatened claw and tooth.

Her eyes, so soft and lonely
To save her, I was doomed
But I did not a monster see
Just a girl wrecked by abuse.

She dragged me to the pit below
I coaxed towards the light
Where we belonged, I do not know
She gashed me with her knife.

'Stop! You're safe.' I forced a smile
Through blood and shocking pain
She walked beside me for a while
Then stabbed at me again.

On the cusp of freedom
She tore my wounds apart
I drew my sword and in defeat
Stuck the blade into her heart.

CROWN OF HORNS

By the ancient dolmen stood
A noble stag with horns aloof
Tines sharp as an arrowhead
So dignified in brown and red.

I leant upon the ancient stone
Said to the deer, 'Guide, take me home.'
Gleaming in a coat of frost
Ice on my lips. 'For I am lost.'

Rings bit my hands, the sky it shook
As through the valley, by the brook,
I followed hooves upon the leaves
Stiff hands reaching for the trees.

Winter's teeth gnawed at my cheeks
Darkness in my breast did beat.
Vicious wolves lurked on the way
The noble stag kept them at bay.

Then upon a battlefield
The stag led to my axe and shield.
With a flush of icy dread
I saw myself among the dead.

Then the voice came as a sword:
'Your courage has a great reward.'
The stag's eyes gouged me deep inside
'You too shall be a spirit guide.'

And thus, I tread the sacred glades
Leaf-filtered light shines on my days.
Please know I am a soul reborn
If you should see my crown of horns.

HARMSPEAR

Atop the sun-dry ziggurat
HARMSPEAR was forged
Early empires rippling
As the Blood God's sword was drawn.

So beautiful a weapon
Its wielder would be Lord.
Bequeathed to divine lineage
While peasants crowed and cawed.

Harmspear sailed the Nile
Anointed pharaohs in his name
Made crypts of mortal labour
Slaves to dynasties insane.

Bequeathed to Xerxes Shahanshah
Harmspear's beak was filled
Bled sands at Thermopylae
Fed by the thousands killed.

History a river,
Tide of corpses in the glade
Harmspear was the crocodile
Hid in the violent shade.

Khans, kings, popes and emperors
Apostles to Harmspear's cause
Youth reduced to bones and meat
The machinery of wars.

Each generation yet seduced
By unconstrained power
Disguised as virtue, Harmspear flies
From another Babel Tower.

Are you are the anointed one
Who'll use Harmspear for truth?
Seduced by your own vanity
Our blood will be the proof.

SKELETONS

The dead loved once,
Though only bones
Speak of their tender sins.

My buried heart
Will be forgotten
When my own life dims.

Sockets dark,
Where once my eyes
Were touched by tearful stings.

While on the wind
Love fleshes others
In her playful whims.

ACTORS

A curtain falls. Our life concludes
We cast aside our costumes crude
And sigh as we decrease.
How hard it was to find some peace.

The script was pain.
Now dead
We reconcile with loved ones
Some estranged.
And cry at the psychology
Our spirits wore:
The clothing strange.

Then it's you and I,
Behind the windy scenery.
A soft, quiet aftermath
Where we can simply be.
So perfect to reside
In your familiar mystery.
No script or mask required
To sail in endless history.

BLACK HOLE

You cannot feel me,
Yet stars die in my cold.
You cannot hear me
Yet my whisper destroys worlds.

You cannot find me,
Yet all things drag in my tide.
You cannot see me,
Yet my force burns deep inside.

You cannot fight me,
Yet I die with nuclear might.
You cannot know me,
Where time slows, I kill all light.

You cannot destroy me
I have died yet grown in might.
You cannot comprehend me,
I was once an angel bright.

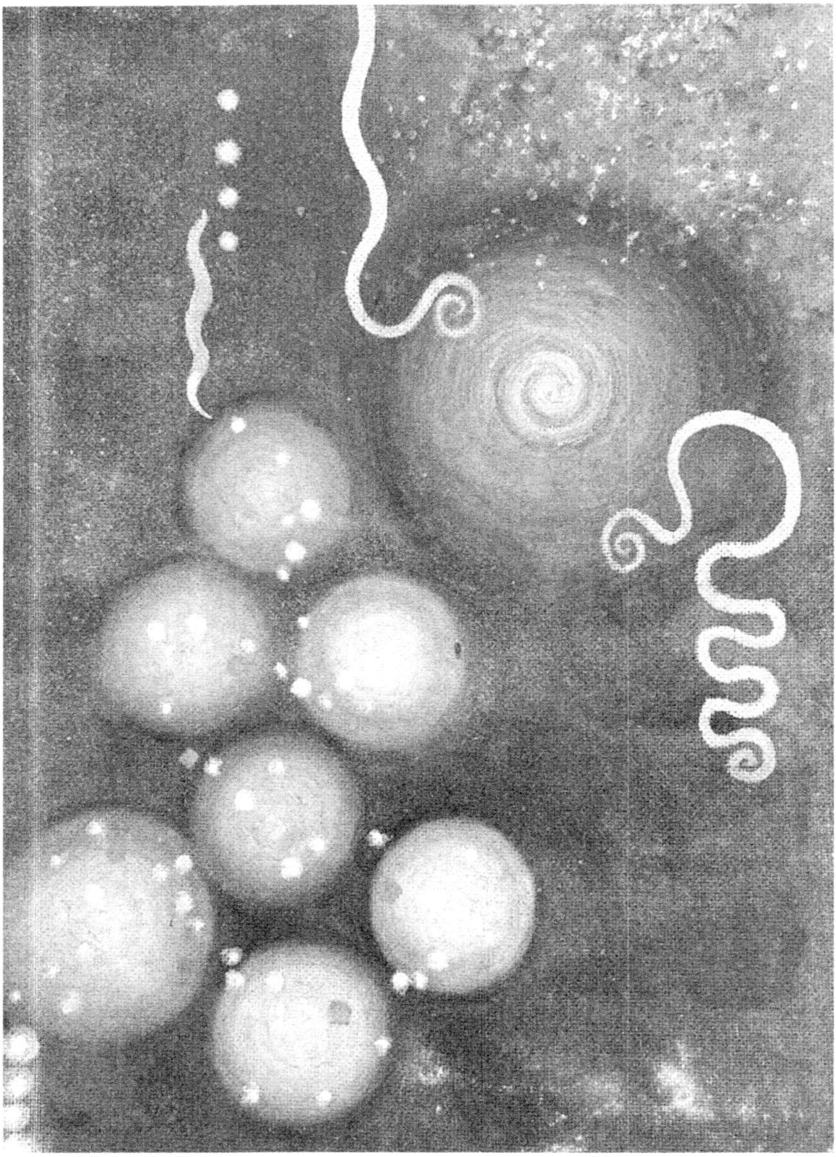

IN THE STILL GALAXY

In the still galaxy
Sophia dreamed of novelty
And fell, in curiosity
Calamitous velocity.

In Sophia's descent
Her spirit rent
Became material and found rebirth
As Gaia-Sophia, the Earth.

As the soul of our world
Our queen and mother
Yearned for her cosmic brother
Far from home, without the other.

Tears became seas
Longing grew reaching trees
And her seeds flung wild
Became humanity, her child.

Deep within your heart
Burns Sophia's longing spark
Lighting the distance
Between the sacred and the dark.

Sophia's cosmic correction
Requires our connection:
To fight against vain powers false
And manifest creative force.

SONG OF SOLITUDE

Slowly trees come into view
From my bed of snow and you
As another dawn survives
Surprised again to be alive.

Rising from the sense of sleep
Whispering dreams and dew touched cheek
A curious sense of darkness lingers
Like the touch of icy fingers.

Setting out on our great quest
I glance behind to see the rest
Trudging forward, eyes are gleaming
But instead of friendly feeling

I sense a growing, lonely gnawing
As if some master plan were thawing
To put us all in deadly blight
Enslave our minds and crush our might.

Although I cannot place the feeling
It seemed to catch me in my dreaming
Reminding me of warning wise:
Who will stand when the Cold Lords rise?

MY LIFE AFTER DEATH

At his grave they celebrated
All the parts of him they hated
Or loved. Or sat in reminiscence
According to their dispositions.

Lowered coffin in the pit
Interred with memories and spit
While in immortal self-assurance
The guests neglect their life insurance.

Time burned on and on
All the mourners now long gone
None recalls their lives, still less
Their flaws or arguments. Their stress.

And though forgotten, unrecorded
Every single word he hoarded
In a stream of consciousness
Unheard but undying, nonetheless.

STRANGERS

Punctured lung, I glisten
So attractive
If you need me to listen
I will gladly lick at your wounds

Sucking the high
Of losing myself
Identity bled out far behind
But I still vampire for more

Stranger, when you speak
I know you seek a priest
Absolution for the sheep
A sacred chore

Only if you hurt me
Can I glimpse my soul's beauty
I am a temple
Wrecked for opening her doors

Stop. Light a candle
Finger wounds in palms and wrists
Share blood for blood
And I will you adore

Then invoke me and I glow
I will give you my email
I will give you my number
I will give you my soul

THE TIDE

Can you hear it?
Surging
Stripping back our lives
Shallow love
So thin it
Gleams off pebbles
Once submerged.

Feelings run dry
Rains refuse to cry
Waves deform and destroy
Blasting cliffside
Like cruel truths
Smashing us until we fall.

Treasure, once
Low in the depths
Made shallow
In this orbit.
With a new moon
The tide takes all it has given.

ONLY VISITORS

Stand upon the world
And beneath your footsteps weigh
The longevity of time and space
Set against internal ache.

The playful cosmic majesty
We alone can apprehend
But our souls, our loaned identities
Are too much for us to tend.

We briefly birth and bloom
Tend a nettle-sting in the heart,
Sprout our nervous love
Then sleep in aeons dark…

MOON

I belong to the distant moon
From her silver seas I swam
Became stranded down below on Earth
Incarnated as a man.

No-one here is like me
Their souls are blue and green
But mine is reflective of nothing
Humans have ever seen.

Loneliness is my natural state
At night I see her face.
I could almost touch it but
It's there in outer space.

Often I wave 'Take me back!'
But I fear she doesn't see
She wanes and when she does react
She shows an eyelid to me.

An alien here, I only found solace
In the oceans, fathomless deep.
I gave up on the moon and on life itself
And simply decided to sleep.

When I awoke, she was glowing
Enormous, round and bright
I had been wrong and I wept for her love
As it lit up the brilliant night.

OF TIME AND A LADY

TIME combs her waterfall hair
Immense in age but fair.
In her painting, she is waiting
Skulls and roses stare.

Counting days in perfect truth
Our years are tears she weeps.
Lady Time in bloom of youth
Trod centuries her feet.

Think on those whose breath
Drew last, in far antiquity.
They loved. To the very death.
Though lost to memory.

Lady Time has caught you
As her comb draws through all worlds,
Madam, see you shine unique
In the slow wave of her curls.

FAMILY

Just as a candle doth soft bestow its light
And cast about its promise, even deeper pools of night
Thus is a whispered knowledge, sweet insight
Cast without sound to make the heart excite.

Shadows like robes may clothe our souls tonight
Sorrows and foes may every moment blight
Yet stars have a constellation, to hope ignite
They do not choose, but know them at first sight.

DAIMONIA - RAIN

Bone Moon, thrown out to sky
Hold me in thy terrible eye.
All our stories performed in your wise glow.
Show me my future! I must know!

Peeling off this mortal dress
Let starlight tickle me with its caress.
I will be an arrow - firing true for thee.
If I can but glimpse the woman I am doomed to be.

On flesh untested, whisper-thin
Splash tears as callous as my sins.
Upon my tongue cruel raindrops spill
I intend to drink my fill.

I pray for such peace and healing
But inside a violent feeling
Wants to leave the whole world bleeding
My true needs I am not seeing.

When the ravens taste my flesh
I'll laugh because I'll be at rest.
No more torturous unrest
Wanting what will hurt me best.

WINTER'S THRONE

Black paints black across the night
Upon the cliffs an eerie sight
A girl with lantern, wind-tossed cowl
And her weapon is her scowl.

Hear the thunder, hear the crows
Girl calm, amid the storm-tossed throes
And the only sound she knows
Is the weeping of her foes.

Stars rain light upon the heath
Pyres burn in the streets beneath
But in her heart - a love like ice
Turns all warmth into a knife.

Achieving now the coldest peak
Girl lets her skin the evening seek.
Hair upon pale flesh and bone
Aloof atop her winter throne.

Yet even the lightning knows
In time she'll gather all her clothes
And yawning, to her home she'll run
Just as snow succumbs to sun.

Around her bed the candles warm
Watch like angels for the dawn.
Melted now, her will to fight
As vengeance dims to morning light.

AVOID MY EYE

I am intuitive. Avoid my eye.
I can see your spirit as you wander by.
I can see the little king who looks down his nose.
I can see the warrior, hiding in a gentle pose.

I can hear the child in the old woman's sigh.
I notice the smiling one who just wants to die.
I can sense the memories more present than the now.
I can feel the future weighing on a burdened brow.

I see the saint who is gripping a gun.
I see vulnerability in the most dangerous one.
I find fragility masked by hostility.
Unsung generosity. Truth and hypocrisy.

I am intuitive. Avoid my path.
I can see the truth of anyone but myself.

THE CURE

If your pain cannot be cured
Through strength of heart or mind,
Redirect to other causes
Find ways to be kind.

Embrace what is provided
Accept the task revealed,
Do the work in front of you
In this you will be healed.

Smashed hopes may remain broken
Lost love never reclaimed,
But do whatever good you can
That's how your heart will change.

THE LAST HUMAN

It's not 'words' which are language
They just fill the gap
Where critical thoughts have relapsed.
Compositions go wrong
Automatic we respond,
Not even making music
Of dead songs.

I am the last human.
I've come unplugged
I dress like a thug.
I snort YouTube videos
Like a mind-altering drug.

Some find me aloof, but I'm just
Wary of proximity.
They provoke my reproof
But I just don't have the energy.
I might even rescue someone if they
Don't get too bloody close to me...

It all ends in tragedy.

Even among neurotypicals
You'll find the cynical.
And those in trauma
Will stare Truth right in the eye
But then ignore her.

I drink a coffee
I purchased with their technology.
I'm wired for inaction
When I see a sight that blinds me:

It's my guardian angel...!
She's so close before I realise
It's nothing like her
Just a reflection
Shining from mirror
To mirror, to mirror.
Faces swapping across miles.
But I guess she's out there somewhere
Avoiding eye contact and smiles.

After dark, I light a fire
Make camp with electric friends.
I'm on my PlayStation, by the way
Not outside. The night
Belongs to the lads
Not to prophets or the mad.
Our place is virtual temples, dank memes
And whatever else they call bad.

I've cut everything in one way
Or another and soon I'll leave
This tomb and roll in green
Forgetting.
Or I could die.
Or go on medication
Swallowing pills in isolation.

Instead, I just write poetry
And wait
For an angelic vision
To decaffeinate my heart
And to send me on my final mission.

FICTION

THE SEA BETWEEN THE STARS

The girl haunted the old tower, after her mother's departure. Neither the girl nor her mother was dead but, like a ghost, the child mourned their separation. Each night she drifted from shadow to shadow, pale feet on stone, hair black as the sea between the stars. When the skies were benign, she was the storm that racked the steeple, torrential in her cries. When all the villagers were asleep, she was their nightmare unravelling in the dark.

Her mother Catherine had not been warm or loving but the girl had learned to survive on meagre pickings, crumbs of unkindness wrapped in concern. She could live for weeks on a scowl or a shrug, almost a month on a single kiss. She found inventive ways to summon her mother's hand to her face, her cheek hot and red from the violent touch.

One night, the girl had watched her mother saddle a horse and depart. 'I hope, one day, you have your own child,' Catherine told her weeping daughter. 'A girl as thankless and difficult as you. Then you'll know.'

The girl already knew. She was unlovable.

Now she chilled the halls of the grotesque tower her family called home, singing to the ravens from the shadows. She damaged tapestries - scratching the faces of kings until stitches became scars. She poured wine over the cats and buried her doll, alive, beneath the earth.

The girl's grandfather -and now parent- would rise from his chair whenever the girl came into the windy hall he drank in. He was a formidable man, once an infamous knight, but hackles rose along his skin as the girl crept into the firelight.

'I'm watching you,' she waved a finger in the old man's face, 'to see if you've been good enough.' She sounded like her mother, but strangely older, callous and crone-like.

The old man's eyes were grey-blue stones, cupped by craggy wrinkles. Those eyes had seen a dozen battles, yet never closed in prayer. They had not blinked when he had dislodged gold from the teeth of dead warriors. They had not wept when his wife was upon the funeral pyre. But they became wide and watery at the girl's strangeness, his black eyebrows rising as he shuddered.

'What's to be done?' Grandfather Jhonan asked the holy men, one white winter morning. He paced the airy hall, rubbing his muscled arms. 'Some evil wears the child.'

'Not evil,' Adjurator Ivan replied. 'Grief wracks her spirit.' His voice became a whisper, forcing the eavesdropping girl to listen intently. 'Many lose their mothers but is it true that Daimonia drove hers away?'

The girl broke from her hiding place, ran past the men and threw open the tower doors.

'Dai, wait!' Jhonan cried, raising a three-fingered hand towards the girl.

She cast a look back at their faces, each was as flush as her own. 'I am death!' she shrieked and ran out into the snow.

The running was heavy, feet sinking into white to reveal lurid green. Daimonia fell against a snow-crowned tree and leaned against it panting. Her nose streamed and fists tightened, the creak of skin rubbing against skin. The day was colder than a reluctant kiss.

Crunching announced her brother Niklos, trudging up behind her. Both their tracks punctured the hill, like wounds on the frosty surface.

Niklos frowned as he approached, his wet hair stuck to his face and neck. 'Mother will come back,' he told his sister.

'Not this time,' Daimonia sniffed. 'I saw something I shouldn't have.'

'Like what?

Daimonia's eyes became small and spiteful. 'Like your girlish face,' she said. Inside her closed mouth, her tongue teased her sharpest teeth. The capacity to hurt was intriguing. To give back a little cruelty for the many cruelties received - it satisfied something growing within.

Niklos sulked then. He had a special face for displaying his pain, one he wore all too frequently.

'What's wrong with you?' he complained.

An ugliness hung in the air. But Daimonia had never seen her mother apologise and it was hard for her to find the way of it. Instead she simply laughed.

Ravens circled above, their caws echoing the girl's cruel mirth.

She found the stone on a summer morning on a day busy with bees and the leafy smell of the forest. It already looked human, sticking out of the brook like the head and shoulders of a drowning man. Daimonia dragged the stone onto the muddy bank, making little heaving noises. She patted the thing's forehead with her palm.

'Wake up,' she told it.

In her room the stone sat by the window, where Daimonia had hefted it. She cupped its head in her hands, taking comfort in its mundane constancy.

By nightfall she was labouring beneath the glaring stars, the tink-tink-tink of her grandfather's dagger chipping away at the stone.

Hammering the blade she cut away all that was inessential, hungry to find the secret within.

A face began to emerge, nose first, then mouth - lips twisted in a sneer of superiority. Daimonia continued stripping the face, releasing it from the primitive rock. Day and night she laboured, keeping the tower awake.

Until she found the face of her mother.

The visage had emerged so gradually that Daimonia trembled to realise what she had created. She fell back upon her bed, looking at the features as if for the first time, so like her own face but with a tip of the neck, a lowering of the brow that implied profound condemnation. So many times she had seen it but only now, in flawless repose, could she wonder at what events might have shaped such sad contempt for the world.

Daimonia curled around the stone, her slender arm reaching across its shoulder, and lay her head upon its head. It was cold, but no colder than the stiff figure she had often tried to squeeze. The godlike face would not leave her, nor offer any reproof. It could not shriek or bare its teeth, nor rip its own hair out in anger. The girl clung to it, as if to a tree in a storm, allowing her heart to enjoy its silent permanence.

Also by Alexander Wallis

The Way Knight: A Tale of Revenge and Revolution
Alexander Wallis
Illustrated by Phil Ives and Anastasia Ilicheva
Audiobook performed by Kathy Bell Denton

When corrupt politicians execute her brother, Daimonia Vornir determines to find her mother – the famous hero who abandoned her years before.

To survive the treacherous journey, she hires THE WAY KNIGHT – a travelling warrior sworn to protect anyone who pays his fee, no matter how dangerous the journey, or hopeless their cause. Together they will chance the battle-torn coast, pursued by the champion of the Secret God.

The Way Knight is the terrifying tale of a girl's journey from child, to woman, to goddess. It is a provocative story that will challenge everything you believe.

Available via Amazon, Kindle and at Audible.com

THE WAY KNIGHT
ALEXANDER WALLIS
'A gripping fantasy novel.
Dark, scary and a total page turner.'
The Wishing Shelf Book Awards
Narrated by Kathy Bell Denton

Alexander Wallis is a community artist who believes that everyone can have a profound experience with art. His earliest work included *Angels of Deception*, illustrated by Ian Churchill (X-Men) and Ian Welch (Starburst) before launching *Elemental* - a cross-generational poetry project, working in partnership with the Chichester Observer and poet Ali M.

Alex's innovative, inclusive approach led to him being commissioned by CAMHS to deliver theatre-based youth work on the theme of mental health. Alex was subsequently employed by Portsmouth City Council to launch and lead drama work which was credible and appealing to teenagers while helping them develop social skills.

Chichester Publishing (and CHINDI) launched Alex's first novel, *The Way Knight: A Tale of Revenge and Revolution,* in 2015. The book was inspired by the experiences of young people grappling with self-doubt in an unjust world and was considered powerful and provocative by reviewers. Alex was subsequently a winner in the *Write Across Sussex* literary competition, presented by world famous novelist Kate Mosse.

Alex continued his community arts work by listening to the experiences of students who had never enjoyed a book. He collaborated with young people to create a story and a narrative voice that would feel true to their issues and perspectives. The result was *I H8 Bullies,* which was published in 2019, and was illustrated by stalwart collaborator Phil Ives.

In 2020, Alex collaborated with poet Nicole Wild to create a series of anthologies, inviting introverts to make loud their thoughts via poetry. *I for INFJ* and *Introspective,* gave voice to the ruminations of reclusive poets from around the world.

Museworks is Alex's first solo poetry compilation and is supported by some of his favourite artists, including Duncan Clarke whose paintings have been treasured in galleries and homes. Alex hopes this book will encourage new writers to try their hand at poetry.

Thank you for reading
MUSEWORKS by Alexander Wallis

If you would like to support this project, please take a moment to review this book on Amazon and let me know your favourite poem!

BloodRedStar

Printed in Great Britain
by Amazon

81958160R00037